Journey
through the Power
of the Rainbow

Journey

through the Power

of the Rainbow

Quotations from a Life Made Out of Poetry

by Aberjhani

ALSO BY ABERJHANI

I Made My Boy Out of Poetry (1998)

The Wisdom of W.E.B. Du Bois (2003)

Encyclopedia of the Harlem Renaissance (2003)

Christmas When Music Almost Killed the World (2007)

The American Poet Who Went Home Again (2008)

ELEMENTAL, The Power of Illuminated Love (2008)

The River of Winged Dreams (2010)

Savannah: The Immortal City (Editor, 2010)

Savannah: Brokers, Bankers, and Bay Lane, Inside the Slave Trade (Editor, 2011)

Visions of a Skylark Dressed in Black (2012)

A CREATIVE THINKERS INTERNATIONAL
AND BLACK SKYLARK SINGING BOOK

http://www.author-poet-aberjhani.com

ISBN 10: 1-312-19411-1
ISBN 13: 978-1-312-19411-3

Manufactured in the United States of America

For Maxine Griffin, Nancy Ann Ellison, and Jacqueline Bradley. Thank you for blessing my life and that of so many others with the extraordinary beauty of your loving presence in this world.

And for the many compassionate citizens of the borderless Internet who inspired the creation of this book.

"We start with gifts. Merit comes from what we make of them."
—Jean Toomer, *Essentials*

"Among all trees, the eternal green pine. Among all landscapes, red stone against a blue sky, with white clouds… And the sea; or better, the feeling that the sea is near…"
—Juan Ramon Jimenez

CONTENTS

Acknowledgments

If anything at all shines new under the sun in these early years of the twenty-first century, it is the hyper-intimate role the Internet has come to play in the daily lives of individuals across the globe. A number of people and organizations with whom I first became familiar through the Internet played a very significant part in the conception and composition of this book. I am as grateful for the unknown hundreds of thousands (or more) who took it upon themselves to introduce friends and communities to my work, via social media such as Twitter, Pinterest, Tumblr, and Facebook, as I am to brilliant entertainment celebrities like LL Cool J and Hill Harper for doing the same.

This book possibly owes the most to the many writers who first dedicated themselves fiercely to their craft and then survived long enough to produce the works, and live the stories, that have inspired me and numerous others to follow in their literary footsteps. Some have been singled out by fame and history to become celebrated figures. Others may be less well known but any quick study of their individual writings will reveal a powerful intelligence carefully at work compiling notable statements and revelations on the wonder-filled complexities of how human beings inhabit life.

I think of the French polymath Boris Vian (1920-1959) who burned the candles of his creative genius at every end he could light. And I think of the way Zimbabwean author Dambudzo Marechera (1952-1987) hammered with furious genius through walls of racial and cultural impediments in the struggle to satisfy his ravenous hunger for freedom and sanity. I consider the dogged determination of Harlem Renaissance great Zora Neale Hurston (1891-1960) to define her art and life according to the vocabulary of her own soul. There is also Henry Dumas (1934-1968) who lost his life to a policeman's bullet, but whose creative passion before that burned true and steady enough to help provide aesthetic direction for such modern-day giants of fiction as Toni Morrison.

There are, as well, those fellow scribes with whom I shared writing workshops, spoken word artists who stood with me on stages in front of microphones, literary neighbors on websites such as Red Room and Creative Thinkers International, and the readers and audiences who continue to bless my work with their valued attention.

Bibliography and Key to Sources

AAC—National African-American Art Examiner Column

AP— *The American Poet Who Went Home Again* (2008)

CMW—*Christmas When Music Almost Killed the World* (2007)

EPL—*ELEMENTAL, The Power of Illuminated Love* (2008)

EHR—*Encyclopedia of the Harlem Renaissance* (Facts On File, 2003)

GFO—*Greeting Flannery O'Connor at the Back Door of My Mind* (manuscript)

GDT—Guerrilla Decontextualization (manuscript)

IMBP—*I Made My Boy Out of Poetry* (1998)

IC—*Illuminated Corners: Collected Essays Vol. 1* (manuscript)

NSP—New and Selected Poems (manuscript)

RR—Aberjhani's Red Room Blog

RWD—*The River of Winged Dreams* (formerly The
     Bridge of Silver Wings)

UCI—Uncollected Essays and Interviews

VV—Visionary Vibes, column published in *Creative
     Loafing News Magazine*

VS—*Visions of a Skylark Dressed in Black*

WD— *The Wisdom of W.E.B. Du Bois* (Kensington Books,
2003)

Introduction

When an acquaintance from a social media site emailed me in March 2011 to tell me a quotation from one of my books was apparently circulating on Twitter as a "quote of the day," I said to myself: *Oh, that's nice, I think.* As a brief afterthought while turning my attention to other real-time matters, I hoped someone would find the quote useful. I learned the next day that the trend had continued. I became curious enough to take a break from my work in progress—a literary memoir with the working title *Greeting Flannery O'Connor at the Back Door of My Mind*—to do a bit of net surfing and look at the quote itself:

> Dare to love yourself
> as if you were a rainbow
> with gold at both ends.

It came from the poem "Angel of Healing: for the Living, the Dying, and the Praying." A kind of rainbow-striped light bulb went off in my head as I noted the poem was part of the original *Songs of the Angelic Gaze* series written in 2006 during what I have come to call *the summer of the angels*. That was the summer following my mother's death after I had served as her caregiver for a decade. As stated in *The River of Winged Dreams*, which contains the entire *Angelic Gaze* series, the summer of the angels was an extremely difficult time and I often wondered about the winged poems that took over my life in ways I never imagined poetry could. That they were meant for more than just me was something I never doubted. Now what had started out as an articulation of ambushed wonder was arcing across the sky of other lives in a very different way with different meanings and effects.

As I understood it, "Angel of Healing" had come to me largely to affirm faith, hope, and determination in the face of violence, disease, and widespread starvation gripping the world community at the time—in truth, as of this writing very little has changed since then. That particular haiku stanza, I had hoped, would speak some faith into the hearts of the 33,300 young, old, and in-between cross-cultural individuals in the United States alone on their way to committing suicide; and to the 20 million, according to the World Health Organization, throughout the Global Village who attempted suicide every year. Whether naïve on my part or not, it seemed worth taking the time to try to convince others that their lives possessed beauty and meaning worth preserving and honoring. I had hoped too that these lines might help persuade those silently combusting inside suppressed rage and muted disappointments to express their painful frustration in ways other than mass murder. If they could recognize and celebrate value within themselves, then perhaps they could allow the same in regard to those upon whom they projected their own self-loathing and sense of worthlessness.

As the full title of the poem suggests, it was a prayer in which grief bonded with humility and longing to claim the agonizing wounds of the era in order to implement recovery from them. The poem is divided into three parts, each of which has generated at least one now well-known quotation. The first part contains a set of four haikus, the second part four aphorisms, and the third another quartet of haikus. Because the poem is as much a howl of 21st-century angst as it is a chant for seemingly overdue relief, it contains certain images which are not likely to become quotes of the day or week but which nevertheless bore witness to the horror of the times. The following haiku, for example, was inspired by a photograph of an emaciated child, in an African nation, attempting to extract food from beneath a donkey's tail:

> Pull the child away
> from feeding at the mule's tail.
> Give the baby food.

When I first shared the poem on the AuthorsDen website, I included within this stanza a link to the photograph but decided the shock of such a graphic disgrace might cause some serious heart issues for some of my more sensitive readers. I also wrestled with qualms over the fact that the photograph had been taken at all and I wondered if the photographer had done anything after getting the image to help the child. I had no doubt the intent behind taking it was to jolt the world's conscience out of its befuddled comfort zones of apathy and into a state of engaged compassionate action. In preparing to post the page on AuthorsDen, I inserted the link and removed it several times before settling on its omission.

If the rainbow quote reflected the need for scarred and abandoned souls to celebrate their inherent value, the quote about the child and mule acknowledged the challenge of sustaining an inner peace unshaken by the chaos erupting throughout the rest of the world. That challenge, however, was one which had to be met before an individual could hope to help humanity make its way from a suicidal faith in hatred and indifference to a more soul-nourishing investment in cooperation and the concept of a truly functional worldwide human community.

II.

After musing over the rainbow quote itself, I decided to take a quick survey of the people who were sharing it on Twitter. What caught my attention immediately was that they were mostly, if not all, attractive young women. That further magnified my curiosity until I started following the trail of who was sharing the quote with whom.

Moving from one cluster of Twitter friends to another, I traced what appeared to be the original tweet back to a profile called The Single Woman, managed by one Mandy Hale, with some half a million followers at the time. I was as baffled as I was thrilled. How had I gotten so lucky as to have my name attached to an online community of so many unattached brilliant and beautiful women? Chances were The Single Woman, or someone connected to her, had originally gotten the quote from the ones included on my Goodreads author profile.

I spent a bit more time looking at some of the blogs and other websites linked to the rainbow tweets. For many of them, the quotation served the singular purpose of intensifying positive motivation already activated in their lives. They waved it like a spiritual banner to remind themselves not to allow failed romantic relationships, disapproving family members, or a lack of support from "established" entities to wreck their self-esteem and prevent them from achieving such goals as graduating from high school or college, starting a new business, or exploring diverse possibilities for achieving happiness.

Some indicated that their lives, which often they equated with the notion of their living souls, had already been brutally damaged by trauma that left them crippled on the inside as well as broken, sometimes, on the outside. They were among the living and praying survivors addressed in the original poem. The seventeen syllables of that simple haiku had become part of the arsenal of mantras they employed to reclaim the joy, and possibly the potential, of which they had been viciously robbed.

My initial intrigue over the Twitter phenomenon likely would have vanished—just as rainbows themselves eventually do once they have delivered their shining divine promise—if subsequent waves of postings had not occurred. Whereas The Single Woman had introduced the quotation to her corner of the Twittersphere in the spring of 2011, later that same year, during Thanksgiving Day weekend, another online advocate for self-respect referring to herself as "SpiritualNurse Sandy" shared the quote with a community following of 38,000. A fellow lover of Rumi known as Pinar Akal added it to her profile in February 2012 and shared it with 50,000 plus connections. The multi-talented spiritual intuitive Beth Layne did the same. You have probably guessed by now that this wave effect continued to grow increasingly stronger.

Things became particularly interesting when "Twitterverse Master" and "Internet Guru" Gary Loper started employing the quote as part of his reoccurring "#JustForToday" and "#LoveFest" positive affirmation campaigns. While honoring the efforts of others to address the traumatizing ecological, economical, and social issues enveloping the world, he made sure his tens of thousands of followers remembered to recharge themselves with essential self consideration. Even with this almost nonstop activity, I still did not realize that a kind of quiet full-blown movement was beginning to develop around the concept until different individuals on various websites began matching the quote with exceptional photographs and original digital art images. Some went so far as to actually create products like cups, t-shirts, posters and notecards featuring the quotes and consequently had to be reminded of the illegality of such actions where a living author's copyrighted work is concerned.

Just how far, wide, and high, I wondered, could this simple haiku transformed into a staple of new-media positive thought possibly reach? The answer started forming when the iconic supermodel Iman Abdulmajid included it via Twitter and Facebook in her *Daily Iman* blog, and American Idol runner-up Adam Lambert shared it with more than 2 million fans. Then, as if the universe were teaching me not to place limitations on the power of the rainbow, a major superstar of television and music shared the words with more than 3 million followers. By doing so, he set off a controversy over the use of social media as a platform for positive inspiration.

The icon in question was LL Cool J, who tweeted the quote early on the morning of February 26, 2013. That one click to millions of followers may very well have had the intended impact of passing positive motivation on to LL Cool J's fans. But it also drew the satirical wrath of *Acclaim Magazine's* Robbie Ettelson. Author of the unkindly-named column, "No Country for Old Rappers," Ettelson published a sarcastic tirade titled "Being Positive is for Chumps" with brilliantly colorful graphic art featuring a bare-chested LL Cool J surrounded by pots of gold and with a huge rainbow in the background. The hilarity of the piece could not be overlooked and prompted this author to respond with the article "This is Why Hip-hop Icons Like LL Cool J Tweet Positive Quotes."

III.

I have always been aware that books and quotations are much like children, who evolve —precisely as nature intends— beyond parental influence to occupy their own place in the world. So for the most part I was at peace watching the excerpt's progressive impact, and even more than that I was astonished that the seventeen syllables of the rainbow haiku had made their way into creation through my pen.

As it turned out, other quotes from my work started to make their way onto the pages of various celebrities' and organizations' profiles. On the one hand, there was television's Judge Greg Mathis on Facebook and Twitter blogs posting "Souls reconstructed with faith transform agony into peace" (Oct 30, 2012). Then there was actor and author Hill Harper tweeting "Hearts rebuilt from hope resurrect dreams killed by hate" (Feb 17, 2013); and Broadway actress Tonya Pinkins sharing on Valentine's Day 2013, "What a lover's heart knows let no man's brain dispute."

When my astonishment grew even more intense, I reminded myself that we are living in an era in which billions of people are grappling to promote communication, tolerance, and understanding over the more destructive forces of war, terrorism, and political chaos that have characterized the beginning of the 21st Century. My Creative Thinkers

International website had been founded to encourage that very process. So I was less surprised than previously when actress and singer Dianna Agron, most notably of the hit television series *Glee* fame, included in a fall 2013 edition of the excellent website *You, Me & Charlie*, one of my quotes on creativity. Doing so made sense enough because the site was designated as "a creative digital playground for users to inspire each other as friends and artists." Moreover, all of the main characters on *Glee* for half a decade had embodied that very concept to much critical acclaim.

Among the well-known individuals who have utilized the quotes, many are affiliated with philanthropic organizations dedicated to alleviating hardships suffered by others. One such organization is *Reach Out Worldwide*. Founded by the late actor and humanitarian Paul Walker, the organization on September 4 featured on its social media profiles a popular quote (also borrowed from the poem "Angel of Healing") on compassion along with a photograph of Walker tending to the needs of a group of children. Walker's own motto for the organization was, "When you put good will out there it's amazing what can be accomplished."

IV.

The one remaining development that managed to blast me all over again with awe was the way usage of the quotes played out on the international stage. The use of some, once I thought about them, was less remarkable than it appeared to be simply because regardless of the flag under which it

occurs, human suffering in need of compassion and relief is
exactly that: human suffering in need of compassion and
relief. But the nature of that suffering in certain regions and
the role assigned to specific quotes proved educational, such
as when anti-racism groups in Pakistan—i.e., *United against
Racism and Ethnic Discrimination in Pakistan*—in Kenya, Mexico,
and elsewhere adopted various quotes reflecting social
responsibility as slogans and "proverbs" during social and
political rallies.

Likewise, the Multicultural Communities Council of South
Australia found what they described as "a quotation for our
times" in lines from the poem "Fulton Street/The Series"
published in *ELEMENTAL, The Power of Illuminated Love*.

In fact, any number of communities pushing for greater
tolerance and celebration of human diversity found different
citations useful. The leading South African newspaper *City
Press*, on July 7, 2013, prefaced a story titled "Lost to
Prejudice," about the brutal murder of 26-year-old woman
named Duduzile Zozo, apparently killed because she was "a
lesbian who made no attempt to hide her sexuality."

Bloggers based in Hong Kong translated into Han Chinese
the poem "Angel of Earth Days and Seasons" to help draw
attention to the problem of air pollution in Asia's rapidly-
growing urban centers. Various readers decided the haiku-
influenced structure of the stanzas made some of them
perfect for stand-alone quotes. In a number of cases, I wished

I had been able to physically participate in these demonstrations for human rights, dignity, and environmental concerns, so was thrilled to enjoy representation through my work.

However, I was more than thrilled when I discovered in 2013 that the visual artist and photographer Jaanika Talts of Dublin, Ireland, had been employing excerpts from my work to accompany her own elegant creations shared with fans on Facebook. She noted that some of these highly-original creations, filled as they were with mythic and archetypal images of women and nature, had first been inspired by the words when she read them on Goodreads. Given the creative enterprises enjoyed previously with such American artists as Gustave Blache III, Luther E. Vann, and Michele Wood, I was moved enough by Ms. Talts' visual interpretations of my words to write *Sensualized Transcendence: Editorial and Poem on the Art of Jaanika Talts.*

At least part of worldwide reading audiences' growing familiarity with my work has to be attributed to the late "King of Pop" Michael Jackson. Although I started writing about Mr. Jackson's life and legacy after in his death in 2009, I did not understand just how many people around the world had been taking note of those writings. Then it was brought to my attention that several full articles had turned up on multiple websites in the form of unauthorized translations into German, Italian, French, Spanish, Greek, Portuguese, and other languages. Given the ease with which Internet technology makes it possible to accomplish such linguistic feats—precision of the translation notwithstanding—I told myself it had been inevitable. Technological ease was only part of the reason. Another very significant part was what I had sensed myself and what author and Minister Barbara Kaufmann had identified as the "spiritual emergency" into which Jackson's fans around the globe had found themselves plunged upon his death. They had discovered little to no consolation within a mainstream media and sideline tabloid press that continued to employ guerrilla decontextualization to sensationalize and capitalize off distortions of the megastar's image even as the worldwide community he left behind flailed about in a tsunami of unrelenting grief. Rev. Kaufmann herself has addressed with exceptional precision, knowledge, and compassion the needs of that community and the seemingly unending complexities that engulf Mr. Jackson's legacy through her *Inner Michael* website and acclaimed *Words and Violence* education project.

In an effort to help balance the often overwhelmingly negative reports (substantiated or not) filed on Jackson, the Argentinian fan group called Blues Away produced a series of digital art images featuring the "King of Pop" with Spanish translations of text from the essay and poem, "Summer-Song Rhapsody for Michael Jackson." These were produced for non-commercial purposes specifically for the MJ Fan community. Because I recognized the difficulty so many had (and which some still have) coming to terms with Mr. Jackson's death, it seemed important to support the alleviation of this particular spiritual emergency in whatever way I could. I therefore welcomed the addition of my text to these digital posters which, like Jackson himself, had gone beyond boundaries of race or nationality to embrace the humanity of those who needed so much to be embraced.

Finally, what may be the ultimate confirmation of the quotations' global attraction came in early 2014. That was when lines from both *The River of Winged Dreams* and *ELEMENTAL* appeared in two online publications created by the United Nations. One was picked up for the *UN News* page after first appearing in *The Barbados Advocate* and the other published in the January 16 edition of the *UN Special* online magazine.

V.

Ironically enough, I had been quite comfortable collecting and editing quotes for *The Wisdom of W.E.B. Du Bois* but found myself baffled at first by the intensified interest in my own. As it turned out, according to friends more techno-savvy than I, the trend known as "microblogging" had boosted the popularity of quotations in general because they provided post-ready content already proven to express thoughtfulness, communicate a specific idea, or reflect a set of circumstances. Love, anger, revenge, creativity, spirituality, betrayal, loyalty, pain, joy, patriotism, victory—were often captured via the appropriate quip from wordsmiths such as William Shakespeare, towering figures of history like Martin Luther King, Jr., or brilliant thinkers like Maya Angelou. Consequently, my *Dare-to-love-yourself* quote suddenly became only one of dozens extracted from the larger body of my work, including four volumes of poetry, a novel, short stories, memoirs, *Encyclopedia of the Harlem Renaissance*, the aforementioned *Wisdom of W.E.B. Du Bois*, author blogs, *National African-American Art Examiner* column, uncollected essays, and other early columns and articles.

It is possible I should have become angry in regard to those website owners who took the liberty of creating entire pages of quotes from my work without bothering to ask permission but my response actually was quite different. I at first was fascinated to realize I had written so much over the course of my twenty-five years as an author and smiled at the fact that the works sampled on the Internet did not even include the hundreds of articles written for the U.S. Air Force.

Secondly, I found myself impressed by the ever-evolving wonder of Internet technology, and in those cases where the quotes had not been illegally employed to advertise a company's commercial products I decided that some websites had done me as well as the reading and blogging public a favor by sharing and promoting the work. And finally, what I discovered inspired me to produce this book, which features a substantially larger collection of my quotations than available on any single website or on the Internet overall.

In one very important sense, *Journey through the Power of the Rainbow* contains the kind of abbreviated distilled insights and results of concentrated intellectual focus developed over a period of decades that readers prefer to find in books of quotations. It is, however, substantially more than that. Taking its cue from the proven fondness for the rainbow quote, the chapters of the book form an arc of human experience that move from meditations on creativity and love to reflections on diversity, time, change, humanity, and hope. At its center is "Tao of the Rainbow," which expands on popular spiritual, mythological, and social conceptions of the rainbow by showcasing a short essay with a collection of primarily original poetic aphorisms never published before.

The book's format allows readers the choice of reading it straight through, accessing with the flip or scroll of a page the subject in which they are most interested, or surprising themselves with random discoveries. From another equally important perspective, *Journey through the Power of the Rainbow* represents a condensed compendium of literary efforts from a life dedicated to transforming the themes of injustice, grief, and despair that we all encounter during some unavoidable point of our existence into a sustainable life-affirming poetics of passionate creativity, empowered spiritual vision, and inspired commitment. Individuals continuously embrace what it has to offer because they recognize that it has already embraced, and celebrated, the beautiful uniqueness each of them have to offer.

Aberjhani
Savannah, Georgia, USA
12 April, 2014

1. Creativity

The Universe said, "Let me show your soul something beautiful."
(EPL, Washington Park #162)

Creative visualization may be described as an extended meditation session that reaches beyond passive contemplation and achieves transformative action. The uses to which it may be applied are limited only to individual imagination.
(VV, Empowerment through Creative Visualization)

Genius begets new creative vision, which often begets new
jobs, which in turn pulls off that much-discussed trick of the
hour: stimulates the economy at one level or another.
(RR, Shining a Bloglight on Two Musical Icons)

At the edge of madness you howl diamonds and pearls.
(RWD, Sunday Afternoon and the Jazz Angel Cometh)

Neither Genius nor Madness ever looks upon the world as a
finished product. Both tend to view it as a kind of work in
progress subject to their peculiarly mesmerizing influence.
(IC, Dancing with Genius, Dancing with Madness)

The validity that society affords art and the value that society
does or does not place upon the lives of creative artists
working in any given medium was very much an issue during
the [Harlem] Renaissance and is very much an issue now.
(UCI, Black Voices Magazine Interview)

Poetry, like jazz, is one of those dazzling diamonds of
creative industry that help human beings make sense out of
the comedies and tragedies that contextualize our lives.
(RR, All That National Poetry Month Jazz)

At the edge of madness you howl diamonds and pearls.
(RWD, Sunday Afternoon and the Jazz Angel Cometh)

Music's sweet labors
give birth to a springtime rush
of sighs rippling dreams.
(RWD, Midnight Flight of the Poetry Angels)

An exceptional mind is a beautiful thing to develop.
(IC, Author Toni Morrison: Writings outside the Fiction Box)

The existence of music itself is reason enough for some of us
to approach each day with an attitude of gratitude but some
of its more accomplished craftsmen and craftswomen
provide us with real opportunities to stop, look, listen, and:
celebrate.
(RR, Shining a Bloglight on Two Birthday Boys)

Art gives its vision to beauty not always recognized. And it
surrenders freely -- whatever power it possesses to every
sincere soul that seeks it. But above all else--it presents us
with the gift of ourselves.
(UCI, Living Poetry, Living Art III presentation Nov 7, 1998)

These twins called Genius and Madness often appear to be the same thing. They both have a tendency to blur the lines of what we call norms, or established reality. They both, when we study that grand tapestry known as history and modern-day society, tend to stand out in much bolder relief than other figures.
(IC, Dancing with Genius, Dancing with Madness)

To create art with all the passion in one's soul is to live art with all the beauty in one's heart.
(RR)

The act of writing itself is much like the construction of a mirror made of words. Looking at certain illuminated corners of or cracks within the mirror, the author can see fragments of an objective reality that comprise the physical universe, social communities, political dynamics, and other facets of human existence. Looking in certain other corners of the same mirror, he or she may experience glimpses of a True Self sheltered deftly behind a mask of public proprieties.
(UCI, A Book Review is a Mirror in Another Writer's Hands)

There's nothing surprising in the observation that literary artists and visual artists often combine their talents to create works which, when joined together, allow each to transcend

possible limitations of the other. The literary artist lends verbal depth to the visual. The visual artist provides visible articulation for the literary.
(UCI, Living Art, Living Poetry)

While it is unlikely that poetry or art shall eliminate the reality of war in the twenty-first century, it is thrilling to know there remain individuals, and even entire communities, still willing to invest in art and poetry's own uniquely explosive contributions to the great, and small, dramas of human history.
(UCI, Living Art, Living Poetry)

The image titled "The Homeless, Psalm 85:10," featured on the cover of ELEMENTAL, can evoke multiple levels of response. They may include the spiritual in the form of a studied meditation upon the multidimensional qualities of the painting itself; or an extended contemplation of the scripture in the title, which in the *King James Bible* reads as follows: "Mercy and truth are met together; righteousness and peace have kissed *each other*." The painting can also inspire a physical response in the form of tears as it calls to mind its more earth-bound aspects; namely, the very serious plight of those who truly are homeless in this world, whether born into such a condition, or forced into it by poverty or war.
(EPL, The Homeless, Psalm 85:10)

Beauty will snatch us by the heart and love us until we are raw with understanding. (IMBP, Calligraphy of Intimacy)

Sometimes the words came like ecstatic utterances, sometimes like songs whispered from another time, like actual angelic possessions, or like mental files that had been downloaded while I slept and then printed via my pen as soon as I got up.
(RWD, Feathers of Gold, Feathers of Silver)

Sometimes: the struggle and willingness to say the unsayable -- has cost poets and artists their lives.
(UCI, Living Poetry, Living Art)

Art, rightly applied, provided humanity with the symbols, insight, and vicarious experience necessary to help one person place him- or herself in the shoes of another, and by so doing come to appreciate the commonality of human experience.
(WD, Love, Art, and Culture)

Literary history contains more than a few examples of writers who followed their literary instincts to notable success and others who followed it to forgotten failure.
(RR, Publishing Options and Consequences)

The reality of a serious writer is a reality of many voices, some of them belonging to the writer, some of them belonging to the world of readers at large.
(VS, Introduction)

It's not uncommon for people who possess certain passions to develop exceptional instincts in regard to the objects of those passions.
(UCI, Authors and Books to Watch in 2009)

The best artists do not attempt to ignore or dream away the horrors of the world. Neither do they wallow in the existence of such soul-devouring terror for its own sake.
(IC, Text and Meaning in Langston Hughes' The Negro Artist and the Racial Mountain)

Creativity by its very nature attracts unclaimed potential and presents it with energy and opportunity capable of reconstructing tragedy into triumph.

(UCI, Creative Thinkers International: A Magnetic Imprint Unique Unto Itself)

2. War and Peace

The same hot lightning that burns your blood with passion—
cools your fears with peace.
(RWD, Poets of the Angels)

For those whose lives are not defined or daily obliterated by
the horrific butchery that characterizes existence in such
places as modern-day Darfur or World War II Nazi
Germany, the word "genocide" comes across as a
sociopolitical contradiction almost too insane to contemplate.
(UCI, Ararat Tells Devastating Story with Power and Style)

The reasons we should want do a lot better may be heard
from one continent to the next screaming, crying, or exhaling
a final breath in communities desperate for peace and sanity.
(GT, Guerrilla Decontextualization and the 2012 Presidential
Election Campaign)

There are those fighting
at this moment—whether poets,
cooks, fathers, mothers,
teachers, students, musicians,
boyfriends, girlfriends,
or something else— who continue
to sacrifice their hearts' desires
 in the name of freedom
and security for others.
(VS, Holiday Letter for a Poet Gone to War Editorial with
Poem)

On faith's battered back calm eyes etch prayers that cool a
nation's hot rage.
(RWD, Midnight Flight of The Poetry Angels)

We absorb just enough of each other to discover
a thousand new ways to love and be loved.
(IMBP, Big Black Man within A Nonsociopoliticohistorical
Context)

How many fears came between us?
Earthquakes, diseases, wars where hell
rained smoldering pus
from skies made of winged death.
Horror tore this world asunder.
While inside the bleeding smoke
and beyond the shredded weeping flesh
we memorized tales of infinite good.
(EPL, The History Lesson)

In a rich moonlit garden, flowers open beneath the eyes of
entire nations terrified to acknowledge the simplicity of the
beauty of peace.
(IMBP, Past Present and Future are One)

Virtually every war throughout history, whether civil or
international, has been fought over conflicts between
assertions of imposed authority and affirmations of individual
or sometimes collective rights. Confirming a civilized balance
between the two has cost an immeasurable
fortune in time, actual gold, and human life.
(UCI, Human Liberty Around the World)

In an era dominated by war, cut-throat politics, and economic
vulnerability, it's easy to forget the power and joy one can
claim with a simple shift in focus.
(UCI, Vintage Vibes and Neo Song Style of Nhojj's SOUL
COMFORT)

Millions cheer the warrior spilling blood across the ring
while the one who stands for peace is ridiculed and shamed.
Must hearts forever suffer from ignorance and greed?
Can bombs heal our souls or set our spirits free?
CMW, The Black Skylark Sang a Prophecy)

Faith in destruction as a means of expressing dedication to
life can only intensify a kind of insanity of which humanity is
obligated to heal itself.
(UCI, Staging a Pre-emptive Strike on the Mind of Terror)

Peace is not so much a political mandate as it is a shared state
of consciousness that remains elevated and intact only to the
degree that those who value it volunteer their existence as
living examples of the same… Peace ends with the unraveling
of individual hope and the emergence of the will to worship
violence as a healer of private and social dis-ease.
(AP, February 15, 2003: The History That Peace Made)

Chaos, loving none
so much as itself, slurps and
spits dead souls like bones.
(RWD, Angel of Hope's Persistent Flight)

In a world gushing blood day and night, you never stop
mopping up pain.
(RWC, Angel of Mercy)

Poets, for the most part, define the transcendent essence of
their human experience by the industries of their pens and
spoken words. Yet in the aftermath of 9/11, many poets
from different backgrounds put down their pens and stepped
away from their open mics to answer the call to war. It was
not a mode of expression most would have preferred.
(UCI, Holiday Letter for a Poet Gone to War Editorial with
Poem)

It is, after all, not only nations
and communities
that need peace so desperately
but individuals divided
against other individuals
and within themselves.
(AP, Feb 15, The History that Peace Made)

Whatever reasoning someone might assign to giving greater
credence to savagery over a fundamental respect for life itself,
the final result is almost never the one imagined.
(UCI, Staging a Pre-emptive Strike on the Mind of Terror)

The enemy, clearly, was the fanged nightmare—
of famine, of war and racism, of rape and terrorism… that
walked in human skin while chomping human heads.
(NSP, How Poets and Words Burn Truth into Love)

In my head this cruel unspeakable truth: that we battled and
we cursed and we spilled each other's blood, we relished our
taste of hell and strangled heaven's love.
(CMW, Eli-Jah)

Life in and of itself is worth celebrating every single day but
the current proliferation of wars and genocide in more than
40 countries makes it clear that our species hasn't quite made
it to that level of spiritual evolution.
(RR, Shining a Bloglight on Two Birthday Boys)

Just as preparation for war is the greatest guarantee of war, so
is failure to respect all of love's divine priorities an invitation–
– to catastrophic sorrows of unspeakable magnitudes.
(NSP, Nuclear Snow in Japanese Springtime)

3. Love and Us

Here is the timeless
mystery that pays no heed
to death's greedy pride.
(RWD, Angel of Christmas Love Shining Bright)

Now come the whispers
bearing bouquets of moonbeams
and sunlight tremblings.
(RWD, Angel of Valentine Days and Nights)

Most people are slow to champion love because they fear the transformation it brings into their lives. And make no mistake about it: love does take over and transform the schemes and operations of our egos in a very mighty way.
(IC, The Soul Letters)

The words 'I Love You' kill, and resurrect millions, in less than a second.
(EPL, Christ Listening to Stereo)

In the face of a world where economic hardships often ground the best of the human spirit into the worst, love provided a pathway into hidden chambers of the spirit where nobility and compassion might be salvaged, resurrected, and made stronger.
(WD, Love, Art, and Culture)

To believe in love: has proven dangerous.
(IMBP, Dogbites and Bitches' Delight)

We brought the Love with us and we keepin' it still.
(VS, Every Hour Henceforth)

Evil is mostly confusion seeking to evolve itself into love.
(EPL, Fulton Street/The Series)

If with all your power you kissed the angel of love, what then
might happen? (RWD, Angel of War)

Love as a spiritual or philosophical principle is worth every
poem, book, song, down-on-bended-knee proposal, legend,
myth and dream ever manifested in its name. Love as a
concrete foundation for an authentically functional
civilization requires the around-the-clock labors of
forgiveness. Without it, Love fails, Friendship fails,
Intelligence fails, Humanity: fails.
(RR, *Forgiveness off the Top of My Head*)

What a lover's heart knows let no man's brain dispute.
(VS, The Golden Art of Dreaming Naked)

Love is our most unifying and empowering common spiritual
denominator. The more we ignore its potential to bring
greater balance and deeper meaning to human existence, the
more likely we are to continue to define history as one
long inglorious record of man's inhumanity to man.
(UCI, America's Future in Black and White, review of Fairy!)

If I say your voice is an amber waterfall in which
I yearn to burn each day, if you eat my mouth
like a mystical rose with powers of healing and damnation,
if I confess that your body is the only
civilization I long to experience… would it mean
that we are close to knowing something about love?
(VS, Coffee Morning Rhapsody)

This fire that we call Loving
is too strong for human minds.
But just right for human souls.
(EPL, Star People)

I insist unrelentingly upon ecstasy and I demand that Love
should have its way with all my Lord's creation. (IMBP,
Miguel Upon the Sand Dunes of Ecstasy and Hell)

An outrageous instinct to love and be loved blinded your
arms to lines of propriety—Women and Men,
Christians and Jews, Muslims and Buddhists, white, black,
red, brown. An outrageous instinct to love and be loved
executed your brain every hour on the hour.
(RWD, Once Was a Singer for God)

Eternity is this holy-fool jazz-tune
composed by Love.
(IMBP, Christ Listening to Stereo)

This is what our love is—a sacred pattern of unbroken unity
sewn flawlessly invisible inside all other images, thoughts,
smells, and sounds.
(RWD, The Comforter on Your Bed)

This world's anguish is no different
from the love we insist on holding back.
(EPL, The Homeless, Psalm 85:10)

Love taught me to die with dignity that I might come forth
anew in splendor. Born once of flesh, then again of fire, I was
reborn a third time to the sound of my name humming
haikus in heaven's mouth.
(RWD, A Poet's Birthday Dance through Fire and Rain 2007)

Aren't you supposed to be all powerful unconditional love or
something like that?
(IMBP, Angels and Shakespeare)

Nothing is quite so important as the time, love, and strength with which we bless each other's lives.

(AP, Acknowledgments)

4. Self-Empowerment

Even when muddy
your wings sparkle bright wonders
that heal broken worlds.
(RWD, Angel of Earth Days and Seasons)

First steps are always the hardest but until they are taken the notion of progress remains only a notion and not an achievement.
(AAC, Dancing to the Paradigm Rhythms of Change in Action)

Human nature is a complex formulation of spiritual ambiguities and biological urgencies than we strive to mold into meaningful experiences that are then referred to collectively as "life."
(GFO, Greeting Flannery O'Connor at the Back Door of My Mind)

The impulse to live life with as much freedom as possible is, arguably, perhaps as basic to human existence as breathing itself. (UCI, Human Liberty around the World)

Leaders get to call themselves leaders because ordinary people empower them to do so.
(IC, Barack Obama and the Message beyond the Photograph)

Course you been hurt. You was born to hurt. What make you wanna forget somethin that important? Power that's worth somethin --real power!--live an' grow from the hurt you feed it. (IMBP, Elijah's Skin)

It is much easier to release the scalding guilt and cutting shame of horrors inflicted upon another than it is to release those inflicted upon oneself. (GFO, Dreams of the Immortal City)

Then came the healing time, hearts started to shine, soul felt
so fine, oh what a freeing time it was. (CMW)

Each star is a mirror reflecting the truth inside you.
(VS, Magnetic Black Towards Light)

Your pain is a school unto itself—
and your joy a lovely temple.
(RWD, Poets of the Angels)

Although shock and dismay can jolt us stupid with pain, they
can also infuse us with knowledge.
(AAC, The Road to Selma's Hell and Back)

Life possesses an amazing array of profoundly sad faces.
(AP, This Mother's Son)

I never preach to others that they should live their lives as I
live my life, or believe in those things in which I believe. I
have, however, often encouraged others to seek personal
sources of spiritual empowerment in order to achieve greater
balance and inner clarity within their lives.
(UCI, Living Poetry, Living Art III)

With my ninth mind I resurrect my first
and dance slow to the music of my soul made new.
(VS, DarkMagusMilesAhead #7)

What can bombs know of the illuminated fields so golden
with heaven in your heart's sacred lands?
(VS, Holiday Letter for a Poet Gone to War)

Passion presented with a greater challenge achieves a greater
goal. (VV, The Sexual Side of Spirituality)

Those who obsess over sex to the exclusion of anything else
tend to develop some very unhealthy destructive
psychological dispositions. Sexual interaction as a gateway to
authentic intimacy can help us to access the spiritual essence
within each other. That's why people in long-term marriages
and intimate partnerships sometimes speak in terms of
"becoming each other." The intimacy strengthens trust,
compassion, wisdom, love, self-knowledge and personal
growth. Sexual addictions, like drug addictions, dilute an
individual's power to function in the everyday world of
employment or family life. And yes, it can de-sensitize a
person in regard to the finer nuances of spiritual growth and
awareness.
(UCI, Poetry Life and Times interview)

You are the man newly arriving at history's worm-ravaged door, the woman whose shadows are salves upon the bleeding breasts of the earth, the infant whose heartbeat floods every harp in Paradise.
(IMBP, Self-Knowledge in the New Millennium)

X.
The thorn is a bridge spanning the muddy depths
of agony and sorrow so that one may on the other side
dance to the drums of the rose of joy.
(VS, Gratitudes of a Dozen Roses)

Know yourself fearlessly (even quietly) for all the things you
are.
(VS, Magnetic Black Towards Light)

5. Poets and Poetry

I place my fingers upon these keys typing 2,000 dreams per
minute and naked of spirit dance forth my cosmic vortex
upon this crucifix called language.
(VS, Sweet Brother Beat-Bop Daddy K—Jack Kerouac)

When a reader enters the pages of a book of poetry, he or she
enters a world where dreams transform the past into
knowledge made applicable to the present, and where visions
shape the present into extraordinary possibilities for the
future.
(VS, Introduction)

Poetry looking in the mirror sees art,
and art looking in a mirror sings poetry.
(RR)

The birth of a true poet is neither an insignificant event nor
an easy delivery. Complications generally begin long before
the fated soul carries its dubious light into whatever womb
has been kind enough to volunteer the intricate machinery of
its blood and prayers and muscles for a gestation period
much longer than nine months or even nine years. For most
true poets tend to be a long time coming.
(AP, Great Old Man Mystical Poet on the Mountain)

One of the great powers of poetry is that it does connect
human hearts and minds and souls with other human hearts
and minds and souls across both time and space.
(UCI, The Certain Ones Interview with Vanessa Richardson)

There are those people who come into the world with an
apparent natural affinity for the conception and expression of
language in poetic terms.
(IC, The Certain Ones Interview with Vanessa Richardson)

Poetry and art nourish the soul of the world with the flavor-
filled substances of beauty, wisdom and truth.
(RR)

A poet is a verb that blossoms light in gardens of dawn, or
sometimes midnight.
(NSP, A Poet Is A Clinton D. Powell a.k.a. Poem for a Poet)

Open mic recitals became a favorite outlet for poets during
the 1990s and grew into a powerful mainstay of popular
literary culture after 9/11. In the midst of war,
world disasters, and political hype, the coffee house
microphone amplified the voice of the individual and allowed
his or her voice, whether filled with sorrow or joy or fear or
love, to be heard.
(RR, An Unexpected End to Silence)

Poetry is both a telescope which brings distant realities closer
and a microscope that enlarges those truths which are
sometimes too small to see but which are every bit as vital as
larger elements. Both a telescope and a microscope. Both a
window and a mirror. And it—poetry—comes from
everywhere.
(UCI, Joyous Day Authenticity or Appropriation)

Aime' Cesaire's "Notebook of a Return to My Native Land,"
one of the great prose-poetry works of the twentieth century,
was parented by not one or two, but three literary
movements: the Negritude Movement, the Harlem
Renaissance, and French Surrealism.
(UCI, Cesaire's Unflinching Vision of the Human Condition)

The music of revelation announces itself to the reader in somber brooding tones or in melodies light as air and one is invited to dance with the most captivating of partners: poetry. (VS, Introduction)

The American identity has never been a singular one and the voices of poets invariably sing, in addition to their own, the voices of those around them. (AP, Introduction Home and the Wanderer)

Rainer Maria Rilke greeted and wrestled with the angels of his *Duino Elegies* in the solitude of a castle surrounded by white cliffs tall trees and the sea. I greeted most of mine in the solitude of a house that still vibrated with the throbs of a singular life that had helped shape many lives... (RWD, hardcover front matter)

That which no other will dare say to us, poetry will say to us. That which we think in silence but fear to speak aloud, poetry will speak aloud. (UCI, Living Art, Living Poetry)

A world without poetry and art would be too much like one without birds or flowers: bearable but a lot less enjoyable. (RR)

More than a method of intellectual calculations, poetry is the voice and language of what is most intelligent, fearful, and loving within us. It will certainly lend itself to our outrage at the world's injustice. And it will sing loudly about the glories of human courage and compassion.
(UCI, Joyous Day Authenticity or Appropriation)

There are many descriptions for what can justifiably be referred to as a poet. or poetry. Of what poetry is or is not. Of what a poet should be, could be, or may be.
(UCI, Portrait of a Poet: The Noble Night of Joy)

Literature first spoke to me through the agency of poetry as a means for bringing into focus a personal existence seemingly condemned, at that time, during my youth, to unrelenting chaos. As a tool for personal reflection and self-healing, it helped to clarify not merely the essential sense of my individual self, but the battered mechanisms of mutuality operating, or trying to operate, between that same self and the more expansive entity we refer to as community.
(UCI, Artist statement circa 1997)

I cannot recall a time when I chose poetry as an activity which might --just might-- help convince such angels as truth and beauty to enter my life. But I can recall very specific and precious hours when poetry made its claim upon me.
(UCI, Joyous Day Authenticity or Appropriation)

Such beings [Poets] rarely result solely from the happy
minglings of human egg and sperm but evolve out of forces
as seductively commanding as the magnetic pulsings of jazz
and as numinously elusive as the whispers of an Ethiopian
priest confirming remembrances with his God in the
bright silence of a small dark hour.
(AP, Great Old Man Mystical Poet on the Mountain)

Stars ink your fingers
with a lexicon of flame
blazing rare knowledge.
(RWD, Poets of the Angels)

Due to the nature of my being,
I knew not better.

Where the eyes of lovers prayed,
I was prone to sparkling joy.

Where the garden of grace blossomed,
star-scented moonlight made me drunk.

Where the oceans of heaven sighed peace,
I flowed into a midnight wave of echoes.

For I was a poem that knew no better,
wandering then, wandering now.
(VS, A Poem that Knew No Better)

6. Barack Obama

The election of Barack Obama to the United States presidency represents more than one man's personal political victory. It also in part represents the triumph of the cultural values, diverse spirituality, and enduring legacies of a people who survived centuries of slavery to emerge as a globally influential and celebrated community.
(RR, The Marketplace, Obama, and African-American Culture)

One thing every elected official encounters sooner than later is the reality gap. It can be defined as the difference between campaign promises and the reality of the process behind achieving such promises.
(IC, Obama, the Tea Party, and the Art of Political Persuasions)

The description of Obama as one manifestation of Martin
Luther King's great dream [became] commonplace in 2008;
but in a lot of ways he is also the inevitable outcome of
Lincoln's uncompromised vision of, and love for, his country.
(IC, The Politics of the Muse and the Light that Never Dies)

Like every U.S. president to run for office before him, Barack
Obama discovered that cultivating a vision of change and
transforming that vision into a tangible reality required a kind
of paradigm dance that many of his fellow political leaders
refused to join on the national level.
(IC, Poetics of Paradigm Dancing in the 2012 Presidential
Election Campaign)

You are neither Christ nor King nor Lincoln. But what you
are is willing, capable, and sincere, there upon a bough of
hope and audacity as branded by history as any have ever
been.
(RWD, There Upon a Bough of Hope and Audacity)

What we do today does not always secure reasonable hope
for tomorrow. Only this time—with the fact of Barack
Obama's presidential nomination—our country had
overcome the odds in a profoundly miraculous way. Like
millions—literally, millions—of others, I was privileged to
bear witness to a gift of history more than 200 years in the

making: it was and it is a moment worthy of joy's sweet and bitter tears.
(RR, Why I Cried When Barack Obama Received the Democratic Nomination for President of the United States)

President Obama appears to me to have elevated and implemented the artist-activist concept to the role of empowered servant-leader...
(RR, Dear James Baldwin in lieu of Dear Barack Obama)

The image of Barack Obama's presence in America's White House has embedded itself in the minds of many young black males—just as that of Michelle Obama has done the same in regard to many young black women— as a living symbol emblematic of very different possibilities for their lives.
(IC, Why Race Mattered in the Re-election of Pres. Barack Obama)

As it turned out, the very quality for which Mr. Obama was ridiculed—his profound eloquence in print as well as in person— has become one of his greatest strengths. It has also by extension become one of America's greatest strengths.
(RR, Poem for a President)

The power of this poet-likely-to-become president first won the world's attention at the Democratic Convention in 2004. Even that event could have been described as "improbable"

but it stands now as a fact of recorded history. Between that
history-making speech and Presidential Candidate Obama's
bestselling books, *Dreams from My Father* and *The Audacity of
Hope*, two things become clear about the power of eloquence.
It is not simply melodious syllables or beautiful fury disguised
as poetic art. In the hands and heart of a sincere individual
seeking to serve the common good, it can represent truth,
vision, and clarity empowered by strength, destiny, and
intelligence.
(RR, Rise of the Poet Most Likely to Become President)

Given the public record of muted responses to many of Mr.
Obama's singular achievements and services to his country,
only one kind of irony seems involved: it is that of some
Americans' choice to pretend no such achievements or
services exist.
(RR, Posted Perspectives on America's 2012 Presidential
Election)

With intent to neither idolize nor demonize the man [Barack
Obama], it seems fair and evident enough to say that the
current president of America is not a leader whose way is that
of violent public outbursts. It appears to be more that of a
warrior-philosopher who practices the art of political
persuasion by authoring acclaimed books, delivering well-
crafted speeches, assembling unified coalitions, passing
historic legislation, signing well-aimed executive orders, and

cultivating a poised but accessible demeanor.
(AAC, Obama, the Tea Party, and the Art of political persuasions)

With its built-in capacity for distorting and manipulating the perceptions and actual experiences of entire populations, guerrilla decontextualization has been something of a constant on virtually all sides of every political fence throughout the 2012 election campaigns.
(AAC, Posted Perspectives on America's 2012 Presidential Election)

His status as the country's first African-American president and the national and international events in which his leadership has played such a significant role have already placed him among the most exceptional presidents in America's history.
(IC, Countdown of 10 Amazing Moments from the Year 2011: No. 2 President Barack Obama)

The fact that an African American sits in the White House at the helm of government in the United States of America on this 150th anniversary of Abraham Lincoln's *Emancipation Proclamation* represents both phenomenal political symbolism and a victory of faith in democracy that should not be lost on any American.
(IC, Notes on the 150th Anniversary of the Emancipation Proclamation)

It represented much more than individual prestige when Mr.
Obama traveled in 2009 to Oslo, Norway, to accept the
Nobel Peace Prize just as it indicated much more when
participants in the Arab Spring of 2011 called repeatedly for
him to officially state his support of their efforts. Dig back a
few years and voices inviting the United
States' participation in anything of consequence were all but
mute.
(IC, Poetics of Paradigm Dancing in the 2012 Presidential
Election Campaign)

Midnight Flight of the Poetry Angels

(complete poem)

**"It was a savage scene, and we stayed there for a long
time, watching life feed on itself, the silence interrupted
only by the crack of bone or the rush of wind, or the hard
thump of a vulture's wings as it strained to lift itself into
the current, until it finally found the higher air and those
long and graceful wings became motionless and still like
the rest."**
—Barack Obama, from *Dreams from My Father*

What once was blood streaks
your face with indigo tears
and lush midnight tunes.

Holding silver hands,
you compose a Tao of art
that heals broken wings.

Lips glow violet,
open to reveal tongues bright
with pearl metaphors.

A speckled halo
handcuffs the world's best liars
to soft dark passions.

Music's sweet labors
give birth to a springtime rush
of sighs rippling dreams.

Out of your mouth rhymes
blossom like warm paradigms
already in flight.

Golden, your songs,
and noble; spinning stars on
their axis of love.

On faith's battered back
calm eyes etch prayers that cool
a nation's hot rage.

Inside these scarred hearts
genius flows incandescent
waves of truth made real.

Hope drowned in shadows
emerges fiercely splendid—
boldly angelic.

(RWD)

Tao of the
Rainbow

7.

In her *Myth and Moor* blog, fantasy author and artist Terri
Windling describes going through a period of depression
when she was fifteen years old and traveling on a bus in
Mexico. Debating with herself about the place God did or did
not occupy in her life, she demanded some kind of reason to
continue exercising any degree of faith in a divinity that
consciously and actively cared about human beings. At the
crucial moment when she was prepared to dismiss any such
faith as futile or possibly delusional, something unexpected
happened:

"The bus turned a corner on the narrow, dusty road, and
a gasp went up from the people around me. Above us, a
rainbow arched through a bright blue, cloudless, rainless
desert sky."

For Windling, the rainbow's sudden appearance came
as an immediate response to a painful need for spiritual
affirmation.

A very popular viral video on YouTube captures an
equally compelling scene. Posted by Paul Vasquez, known as

the Rainbow Warrior "Hungrybear9562" or "Yosemitebear,"
the video was published on January 8, 2010. It records the
narrator's to suddenly seeing a double rainbow arced across
the landscape in Yosemite National Park, California, where
he was living. Viewers do not see the narrator himself. They
only see a rainbow that actually appears nearly faded at points
in a video of homemade quality. The intensity of the viewing
comes from hearing Vasquez's unedited reaction to the
unanticipated appearance of the rainbow. About halfway
through the three-and-a-half- minute video, you hear his
emotion-charged voice undergo a powerful shift, from
struggling to describe the rainbow to suddenly giving in to
uncontrollable sobbing.

For those able to recognize such things, Vasquez has
clearly been overcome by a state of spiritual ecstasy that
prompts him to weep out loud, "What does this mean?!"
Interestingly enough, a Wikipedia entry on the videographer's
experience, titled "Double Rainbow," describes his response
as a "Stendhal syndrome-like reaction." Some commentators
on his YouTube blog have suggested his emotionally raw
response meant he was "stoned" or otherwise mentally
impaired. To this—in addition to posting videos providing
his own explanation of what happened— he has responded
with a quote from scripture in the *English Standard Version
Bible*: "Acts 2:12 And all were amazed and perplexed, saying
to one another, 'What does this mean?'" In the traditional
King James Version, the verse reads as follows:

"And they were all amazed, and were in doubt, saying
one to another, What meaneth this?"

Vasquez, or Yosemitebear (as he seems to prefer)

could just as easily have pointed to the more famous passage of Genesis 9:12-16, in which God proclaims the rainbow as "a token of the covenant between me and the earth."

The scientific explanation for rainbows is well-known and wholly plausible. Simply put, light passing through moisture in the earth's atmosphere acts like a kind of natural prism that splinters and bends into a curved alignment of multiple colors, such as violet, red, orange, yellow, and green. Also well-documented is our understanding of what makes visual perception of surrounding environments possible. Light reflecting off various objects enters the eye through the pupil and undergoes a complex yet instantaneous process of visual refinement as the cornea, retina, optic nerve, and brain all combine information to give one's perception some form of coherence. Or meaning. What science cannot explain conclusively is why the known laws of physics and biology that create natural phenomena exist in the first place.

Vasquez's and Windling's experiences both demon-strate the power of rainbows to dismantle presumptions, reconfigure moods, and generate empowering motivation. Even people who are not particularly spiritually inclined give rainbows their attention when they appear and may reflect upon them as potential indicators of some act of grace or a significant change in potential developments. Without unleashing the power of life-destroying missiles or forcing obedience to a particular law, rainbows dissolve preoccupation with the predictably ordinary and encourage belief in the extra-ordinary. Such belief, such inspiration, provides much more than passive hopefulness. Authentic inspiration endows individuals with mental or spiritual energy which they are then able to transform into positive action. It can make all the difference between a man, woman, or child allowing despair to permanently paralyze any dreams they may have for their lives, or, exercising sufficient strength of will to make those dreams a reality.

From 1997 to 1999, I was still working as a bookstore manager, putting in ten to twelve hours per day, five or six days each week, while also serving as a caregiver for my mother. My salary was just enough to handle house expenses and pay someone else to sit with my mother while I was at work. Once I returned home, I would pick up where the healthcare assistant left off and switch from my role as a hard-laboring bookseller to that of a live-in nurse. Very little time, or energy, remained to pursue my goal to become a professional author.

One night I went to bed with the weight of hopelessness more heavy upon my chest and shoulders than usual and it was still there when I got up to go to work the next morning. After checking on my mother to make sure she was not in any kind of distress and would be comfortable until the assistant arrived, I opened the front door. The moment I stepped onto the porch, I saw above the trees lining the southern horizon a rainbow with brilliant wide bands of color. Its radiance was so powerful that I thought for a moment that I was looking directly into the sun and immediately raised my hand to shield my eyes. The unexpected shock sent a wave of tingles across my scalp and down my spine. As I lowered my hand and stared at the unyielding incandescence, I felt like my soul was re-entering my body after a long inexplicable absence. I nearly asked to be forgiven for something but was not sure what I had done that required forgiveness and could not say who I was begging to bestow such grace.

When I arrived at my job, a co-worker asked if I had seen "that giant rainbow across the sky this morning?"

I said I had.

"You know what a rainbow like that one mean? It mean something good gettin' ready to happen."

And she was right. Between the smile that accompanied her enthusiasm and the sheen of assurance which filled the hours that followed, it did indeed turn out to be a very good day.

My stone boots crumbled
and I sat with crossed legs
upon a carpet of painted flame,
rainbows pouring through my hands
like sweet wounds of grace
bleeding peace for all this world to see.
(VS, The View from Where We Love)

After placing a ring of silver moonlight on the Earth's green finger, Heaven made a golden vow and keeps it every time a rainbow appears, declaring "I love you, I love you," and then again: "I love you."

Unless you are here:
this garden refuses to exist.
Pink dragonflies fall from the air
and become scorpions
scratching blood out of rocks.
The rainbows that dangle
upon this mist: shatter.
(IMBPM, Blood and Blossoms)

The language of the rainbow is a lexicon of light devoted to concepts of faith, unity, hope, endurance, and joy.

Rainbows introduce us to reflections of different beautiful possibilities so we never forget that pain and grief are not the final options in life.

Shine your soul with the same egoless humility as the rainbow and no matter where you go in this world or the next, love will find you, attend you, and bless you.

A more complete rainbow is not the half circle which most are accustomed to see curving from one end of the horizon to the other. A full rainbow is not so much a bow as it is a circle, or a finely-tinted halo, that quietly refutes any limitation you might insist upon putting on the universe or yourself.

A part of the rainbow's eternal miracle is that it is at once brilliantly singular and profoundly inclusive.

Rainbows give themselves to everyone without the least amount of prejudice or discrimination.

The sudden appearance of a rainbow can take your breath away as sharply as an unexpected kiss and leave you even weaker with the astonished joy that follows.

A rainbow is a painted song God sings to our souls to remind us that no matter the traumas, terror, or agony of a given moment, we are loved.

There is no envy, jealousy, or hatred between the different colors of the rainbow, and no fear either because they each exist to make the other more beautiful.

The pot of gold at the end of the rainbow is that glow of memory, which continues to hum like a star inside your heart, after the rainbow has gone.

Rainbows give themselves to everyone without the least bit of prejudice or discrimination.

Before it ends, the worst storm in a life rattles your bones with the thunder of pain and shocks your heart with the lightning of fear. Like a divine mad artist it smashes together colors on the canvas of the ceiling of the sky as it prepares to paint a masterpiece in the form of a rainbow. It goes crazy for a while, completes its work, then steps out of the way and says, "There, see? The greater the effort the greater beauty."

The way rainbows shine in puddles of oil should remind you
that hope is a persistent angel who can find you anywhere at
any time and give you the strength needed to defeat despair.

It is difficult to force your heart to stop gazing at a rainbow
because it contains all the harmony and balance you desire to
love in humanity but don't always find there.

The rainbow is a genius that has bestowed upon humanity
numerous gifts: children whose conception was inspired by
its wordless song; scientific theories that helped advance
technological proficiency; accomplished poets, artists, and
madmen who fed on nothing but its promises; and tears of
joy that replaced screams of terror.

Composers have gone mad trying to create symphonies as
equally bold, sublime, and affectionate as the rainbow.

Love is the music to which the colors of the rainbow
endlessly dance each flowing joy and fire through the other,
vibrating grace that angels gather like honey.

To see what dreams look like once they take root in the soul and grow into blossoms of realization, look at a rainbow.

Dare to love yourself
as if you were a rainbow
with gold at both ends.

8. Michael Jackson

Jackson's challenge was to survive for as long as possible the fickle prickly embrace of fame, the raging firestorms of controversy that all but devoured his entire being, and his own attempts to give as much of himself to the world as possible.
(UCI, Writing the Year 2009 Michael Jackson Legend)

Jackson was largely the inheritor of cultural gifts passed down from such masters of showmanship as soul music icon James Brown, all-around celebrated entertainer Sammy Davis, Jr., and famed Harlem Renaissance star Bill "Bojangles" Robinson. He was also a son of his mother's faith and his father's ambitiousness.
(AAC, Looking at the World through Michael Jackson's Left Eye)

If Michael Jackson's life was one that helped to define a musical era ranging from the late 1960s to the New Millennium, his death, now ruled as a homicide, has become one of the definitive events of 2009. It was the one occurrence to halt the intense nonstop media scrutiny of U.S. President Barack Obama's every utterance, whether official or personal, and gesture.
(AAC, *A Moonwalking Giant Lies Down to Rest*)

To speak of Jackson's voice is to speak of more than the acoustic timbre that radiated like vibrating sunlight from his lungs and heart and throat. It is to acknowledge that quality of genius for giving, living, serving, teaching, loving, exemplifying simplicity, and creating— that comprised the essence of everything he strived to become.
(IC, Summer-Song Rhapsody for Michael Jackson Editorial with Poem)

Because his living presence became such an uncommonly global one, [Jackson's] ministry reflected universal ecumenical principles dressed up in ultra-modern dance grooves, love songs to nature, lyrical eulogies in the form of musical elegies, and sermons sung with passionate intensity and suffering eloquence. (AAC, Work and Soul in Michael Jackson's This Is It)

Whether certain interested parties liked him or disliked him, they enjoyed slicing off whatever piece of his fame they could claim for their own.
(IC, Guerrilla Decontextualization and King of Pop Michael Jackson)

However the world community chooses to interpret it, where Michael Jackson himself is concerned, if the purpose of a legacy is to help make the world a richer, more fulfilling, and more humane place than it was during one's lifetime, he can rest in peace knowing he did exactly that.
(IC, Michael Jackson, Legacies of a Globetrotting Moonwalking Philanthropist)

In comparison to the pace of most of our lives, MJ lived at a vibration close to the speed of light. Or at least his creative consciousness vibrated at such a frequency. People like that are hard to fully comprehend at a single glance.
(AAC, Commentary on Summer-Song Rhapsody)

Xenophobia—
you banished with a moonwalk...
danced hate into joy.
(RWD, Notes for an Elegy in the Key of Michael)

While many people like the idea of exercising unconditional love, most eventually find it too draining and impossible to sustain, often because the attempt to practice it is misunderstood, discouraged, brought under attack, or made a target of willful abuse. As sad as it may be to admit, in our modern world people are far more accustomed to hearing news of war, genocide, murder, disasters, famine, and disease than they are to hearing anything about acts of love or grace.
(UCI, Michael Jackson and the Power of Numbers)

"Heart" was something Michael Jackson had by the tons.
(AAC, Looking at the World through Michael Jackson's Left Eye)

A horn of plenty
spills from your hands into the
starved lives of millions.
(RWD, Notes for an Elegy in the Key of Michael)

Summer is the season when the sun reaches its zenith, its peak, when it burns the hottest and shines most golden for the longest days of the year. During this period, it embraces everything with its light, spreads a blanket of reassuring warmth, induces fertility and growth and regeneration, and even causes rainstorms to balance its own overwhelming power. Michael Jackson was very much like that with an abundance of creative spiritual energies that enriched,

inspired, and empowered the lives of more human beings than anyone can accurately count.
(AAC, Michael Jackson and Summertime from This Point On)

Popular culture itself, mainstream media, and segments of society in general feasted on Jackson's seemingly larger-than-life personality and talent in a number of unhealthy ways. Scandal is often far more profitable than integrity.
(IC, Guerrilla Decontextualization and King of Pop Michael Jackson)

Speaking on the Larry King radio show the night of Jackson's funeral, author and spiritual philosopher Deepak Chopra bluntly described him as "a mythical being" and "an ecstatic soul."
(AAC, Work and Soul in Michael Jackson's This Is It)

The beautiful thing about true genius, such as that which Michael Jackson possessed, is that it can inhabit and express its truth in meaningful ways through many forms.
(AAC, Michael Jackson and Summertime from This Point On)

A lot of tabloids, magazines, websites, radio stations, entertainment personalities, and retail chains made tons of good hard cash peddling before the world what they presented as Michael Jackson's eccentricities and possible moral failings. Perhaps now that he has left the stage for the last time, they can pay a bit of that forward by leaning in the opposite direction and honoring the brilliance of his dynamic artistry, the beauty of his dazzling creative passion, and the simple sincerity—however wounded it may have been—of his love for his fellow human beings.

(IC, To Walk a Lifetime in Michael Jackson's Moccasins)

Your lungs must have been
two harps for the way they flowed
music through your skin.

(RWD, Notes for an Elegy in the Key of Michael)

It's possible that the inscription on the Bollywood Humanitarian Award that Jackson received in 1999 sums up what drove the beloved icon to work so hard in order to give so much: "Though he comes from the young American tradition, Michael is the embodiment of an old Indian soul. His actions are an expression of the philosophy of Weda, which asked to work for the people - not for one's own interests.

(AAC, Michael Jackson, Legacies of a Globetrotting Moonwalking Philanthropist)

Summer-Song Rhapsody for Michael Jackson
(Aug 29, 1958-June 25, 2009)

(complete poem)

Summertime opened like a myth spun from gold,
delivering your talent through ages of classic genius
to plant the seeds and nourish the beauty
of all the bright wonders that would color your dance.

Is any path so demanding as that of living a miracle?

Like a cosmic gymnast on a beam of uncommon grace,
or a swimmer slicing through waves of childhood tears--
you transformed fortitude into Olympian triumph.
Hid your hard-won treasures inside the hearts of all who
      loved you.

The more sincere the soul, the heavier the cross endured.

Your voice strung notes like pearls of sky-blue hope
around the trembling throat of humanity's crimson agony.
Upon the heads of those abused and disinherited
your song placed crowns of inspired revelation.

There is no faith so perilous as faith in love.

Summertime blossomed fields of rose-scented dreams—
      and death amplified your sudden absence with new life...

to plant the seeds and nourish the beauty
   of all the bright wonders that colored your dance.
(AAC, Summer-Song Rhapsody for Michael Jackson Editorial
and Poem, MJ Birthday 2012)

9. Spiritual Intuition

You were born a child of light's wonderful secret— you
return to the beauty you have always been.
(VP, Holiday Letter for a Poet Gone to War)

The death of a dream can in fact serve as the vehicle that
endows it with new form, with reinvigorated substance, a
fresh flow of ideas, and splendidly revitalized color. In short,
the power of a certain kind of dream is such that death need
not indicate finality at all but rather signify a metaphysical and
metaphorical leap forward.
(RWD, Evolution of a Vision)

Are there any who fall, when they fall, quite so hard as angels do?
(UCI, review of Gabriel starring Andy Whitfield)

Everywhere we shine death and *life* burn into something new.
(ELP, Star People)

What is this slow blue dream of living,
and this fevered death by dreaming?
(VS, Up on Passion's Rooftop)

Compassion crowns the soul with its truest victory.
(RWD, Angel of Healing)

Love, Mercy, and Grace, sisters all, attend your wounds of
silence and hope.
(RWD, Angel of Gratitude)

Oh what a wonderful soul so bright inside you. Got power to
heal the sun's broken heart, power to restore the moon's
vision too.
(CMW, Soul of a Black Skylark Singing)

At its most dynamic, faith evolves into powerful applicable knowledge.
(VV, Touring the Astral Way)

Feet sandaled with dreams
tread paths of vision leading
to wisdom's sharp peaks.
(RWD, Poets of the Angels)

To disturb the universe does not have to mean destroying the universe. It can mean surprising the stars and ourselves by honoring it.
(IC, J. Alfred Prufrock's Universe Disturbed)

Quote words that affirm
all men and women are your
brothers and sisters.
(RWD, Angel of Healing)

Death is as much a part of life as living itself.
(IC, Countdown of 10 Amazing Moments from the Year 2011: No. 5 those now departed)

By consciously meditating upon spiritual truths and cultivating personal integrity, one need never fear negative circumstances.
(VV, The Power of the Aura)

What hell condemned, let heaven now heal.
(VS, Bright Kiss of Insanity)

If it wasn't for all those silver wings spread out to help you
on your journey, you would'a been dead or someplace
screamin' in a nut house a long time ago.
(RWD, Feathers of Gold, Feathers of Silver)

When the will to learn from the ordinary is present, a seeker
may indeed gain entrance into levels of awareness that are
extra-ordinary.
(VV, Seeking Guidance on the Path)

Silence brings us new names
new feelings and new knowledge.
Dreams dress us carefully
in the colors of power and faith.
(IMBP, In a Quiet Place on a Quiet Street)

Upon the lips of babes asleep I saw light embracing light and
so allowed my syllables to rest there as a prayer they might
sing in their dreams...
(VP, A Poem that Knew No Better)

The ultimate qualifier of any individual's faith is his or her personal relationship with God.
(IC, Remembrance and Healing in Selma)

Un-winged and naked,
sorrow surrenders its crown
to a throne called grace.
(RWD, Angel of Valentine Days and Nights)

Whether one considers dreams a favorite food of poets or an endless chain of enigmas, there's little doubt that they are among the more dynamic indicators of what we call spiritual reality.
(VV, Dream a Little Dream)

If life is a birthday cake
let my face be smeared
with its icing of cognac and kindness.
(VS, In Regard to a Poet's Birthday)

With its leaves so rich and heavy with elation and its crimson face made brighter with visions of divinity the shadow of a certain rose looks just like an angel eating light.
(VS, Gratitudes of a Dozen Roses)

10. Diversity and Multiculturalism

You are the hybrids
of golden worlds and ages
splendidly conceived.
(RWD, Poets of the Angels)

We are born in states of division, set asunder from one
another by geography, language, belief, history, human
weakness, human greed, and human fear. The salvation of
humanity would also be the glory of humanity: to heal the
bleeding division of [its] collective spiritual being by
overcoming the [artificial] differences we inherit at birth.
(AP, With Love a Letter from Yesterday to the Present and
the Future)

Got just enough room to be a friend of yours. Oh I hope you
got room to be a friend of mine.
(CMW, Just Enough Room)

Not a song of yourself but one
of many selves do you sing—
unity embracing multiplicity giving
glorious birth to individuality…
(IMBP, Self-Knowledge in the New Millennium)

The fate that condemns or saves one sooner or later often
condemns or saves another.
(IC, Poetics of Paradigm Dancing in the 2012 Presidential Election
Campaign)

The ultimate test on the way to establishing an ideal
civilization encouraging ideal human behavior was to look
bravely beyond gender, color, ethnic origin, religious
difference, and class distinctions to discover and honor the
value of each unique individual.
(WD, Civilization and Human Nature)

History is a hermaphrodite with many distinguished lovers.
We are neither mysteries nor strangers but the living breath
of revelation made flesh by the unrestrained desires of a free
and universal love. Universal me. Universal you.
(ELP, The Past Present and Future are One)

Your skin is human-hued and tiger-striped.
Your software likes the contradiction.
(RWD, Sunday Afternoon and the Jazz Angel Cometh)

A specific social identity makes for a fairly sturdy
psychological crutch and saves us from having to deal with
the reality of our true selves.
(IC, Letters of the Soul)

If knowledge truly is power, then learning as much as one can
about the cultural migrations and cross-cultural currents that
have shaped the modern world may be just what humanity
needs at this point in history to establish greater harmony
both between various demographic groups and within
individual groups.
(AAC, International Year Celebration Gets Boost from
Hillary Clinton)

Churches, mosques, and various centers for meditation do
not receive the billions of dollars supporting their dedication
to spiritual intelligence that armed forces receive in support
of their dedication to military conflict, helping to make faith
in mass murder and destruction more widespread than faith
in mutually sustained unity among human beings.
(AP, The History that Peace Made)

African Americans, Anglo Americans, Hispanic Americans,
Native Americans, Asian Americans, Gays, Straights, Jews,
Muslims, Christians, First-time Voters and Old-Time
Veterans all stepped forward at the polls to flex their
collective political muscles in numbers never before seen.
From the sleepy back yards of suburbia to the hip-hop streets
of urban America and the labored fields of rural communities
stretching from the Atlantic Coast to the Pacific, ordinary
everyday people decided they were powerful enough and
significant enough to make a difference in our world.
(RR, Blessings Received and Thanks Given, Americans Rock
the Vote)

The way out of the maze of whiteness and blackness that led
inevitably, repeatedly, to violent conflict was through the
simple recognition of and respect for blacks and whites as not
two races but one: the human race.
(WD, Whiteness and Race Relations)

Beneath the armor of skin/and/bone/and/mind
most of our colors are amazingly the same.
(EPL, Fulton Street/The Series)

Are the qualities inherent in a woman's love necessarily more
capable of sustaining life than those inherent in a man's? And
if so, why? Moreover, what personal sacrifices or changes

must men make in order to generate a more life-affirming sensibility? What are the likely consequences--social, individual, political, spiritual--if men fail? And mostly, to what degree, and why, do women so often participate in their own oppression?
(UCI, Love on a Collision Course with Evil)

The first half of the 20th century in the United States and much of the world was an era when racial and ethnic differences determined even the most uncontrived actions. Stepping into a restaurant, boarding a train, engaging in sexual relationships, or running or voting for a public office were all ruled by notions of differences between groups.
(WD, History and the World)

A strategic use of black culture could help generate a more efficient use of American democracy, and democracy more effectively practiced could then produce a genuinely spiritual nation of people. —(EHR, Author's Note)

The experience of repeatedly enduring rejection [when applying for employment] and other affronts based on one's ethnic origins, rather than on a lack of qualifications, can result in what Nkechi Madubuko describes as "Akkulturationsstress." A common term used in English is "culture shock," which may sound comical to some ears but which can lead to crippling states of psychological depression,

delusion, drug abuse, and violent behavior.
(IC, Report on 2011 International Year part 3: In the land of
Afro-Germans)

Racism is any action motivated by racial difference resulting
in a detrimental impact on the life of another individual or
group of individuals.
(UCI, All that Jazz, Connect Savannah)

I split the atom of my European Self… I split the Adam of
my African Self… I split the atom of my heterosexual Self…
I split the atom of my gay Self, of my Christian Self, of my
Jewish and atheist and Muslim Self, I burned the Adam of
my male Self and female alcoholic Self, my poor and rich and
black and white and old young gorgeous fucked up hurt that's
too bad: Self. I fused together every particle that looked or
smelled like truth, and that is who I took to be my lover.
(IMBP, Splitting the Adam)

Once human beings are separated from the context of their
individual dignity, it becomes relatively easy to think in terms
of depriving them not just of their particular identity but of
their personal power as well. And personal power can take
many significant forms, which means it can be destroyed in
many different ways.
(GD, 47 Percenters and Guerrilla Decontextualization)

11. Cultural and Historical Icons

The men and women of the Harlem Renaissance made up a kind of peaceful army of agents of change. Their creative genius as literary artists, musicians, visual artists, social theorists, educators, and political leaders helped move the world forward from times of war, oppression, and poverty, to times of greater political cooperation, racial equanimity, and economic growth.

(IC, The Approaching 100th Anniversary of the Harlem Renaissance)

Among the lessons we can learn from [Abraham] Lincoln's persistent pursuit of positive change in his lifetime is that sacrifice for a noble cause is worth it not only for the moment at hand but for the generations and years to come.

(IC, Notes on the 150th Anniversary of the Emancipation Proclamation)

The grace with which Kafka navigated chronic illnesses, held down a demanding job as an insurance claims administrator, pursued serious literary ambitions, and addressed with compassion the needs of others, made him appear more than human in the eyes of some. That his biological clock seemed to stop around the age of 20 did little to persuade them differently.
(IC, Franz Kafka's Noble Nightmares and Reasons)

Where his musicianship is concerned, Rollins has been lauded for an uncanny ability to improvise nonstop for performances lasting ninety minutes or more. As an individual, he has been applauded for the conscious choice not to allow the drug abuse that destroyed any number of his contemporaries to do the same to him.
(IC, Countdown of 10 Amazing Moments from the Year 2011: No. 6 Jazzmaster Sonny Rollins)

As a talk show host, Winfrey allowed millions to share in the sense of intimate rapport established in interviews with such iconic figures as Maya Angelou, former president Bill Clinton, Whitney Houston, Michael Jackson, John F. Kennedy Jr., Maria Shriver and her mother Eunice Kennedy Shriver, Toni Morrison, Barack Obama, Sarah Palin, John Travolta, Tina Turner, and virtually every "A-Lister" in a given field of the cultural arts.
(IC, Countdown of 10 Amazing Moments from the Year 2011: No. 1 Oprah Winfrey)

By striving so mightily to accomplish specific goals on behalf of one segment of humanity, she [Toni Morrison] went beyond them to create literary wonders capable of enriching the lives of not just her own people, but of all people.
(IC, Author Toni Morrison outside the Fiction Box)

The serious literary author… still obtains some degree of notable status when he or she wins a significant award but their influence is generally restricted to academic environments, Internet literary communities, or various geographical regions. It would be virtually impossible for a modern author to achieve the level of prestige and actual power [Ralph] Ellison commanded based on his intellectual gifts and pronouncements alone.
(IC, The Enigmatic Genius of Novelist Ralph Ellison)

The fact that the mystery O'Connor's life and work continue[d] to draw increasing attention in 2011 is amazing when considering how steeped it is in the language of her times—the very racially charged South of the mid-1900s—and when noting her early death from lupus at the age of thirty-nine.
(IC, Events, Books Highlight Flannery O'Connor Legacy part 2: A writer's life and times)

Some have speculated that the way Camus died made his theories on absurdity a self-fulfilling prophecy. Others would say it was the triumphant meaningful way he lived that allowed him to rise heroically above absurdity.
(IC, Text and Meaning in Albert Camus' The Myth of Sisyphus)

He [W.E.B. Du Bois] was at once a scientist in his skillful use of history as a tool for comprehending the present, and a prophet in the application of his gift for analyzing the present as an indicator of the future. Because he lived both firmly entrenched within his time and decades ahead of it, the light of his wisdom, like that of his great love for humanity, is one that never diminishes.
(WD, Introduction)

A very shrewd observer of subtle oddities, Alexander unearths the comic and tragic ambiguities of the human condition, allowing us to alternately laugh at ourselves, cry for ourselves, and stare in awe at the beautiful complexity of what it means to be human.
(IC, Review of Inaugural Poet Elizabeth Alexander's Body of Life)

His [Ben Okri's] work poses very serious questions for the twenty-first century. Among them: To what extent will we

allow the indefinable dynamics of something called "destiny" to maintain grief and horror in the world? How hard are human beings willing to fight to achieve and sustain justice, equanimity, or joy? And should progress be called such when it devours what is best within the human spirit?
(IC, Ben Okri's Famished Road Leads to Thrilling Adventure in Reading)

Sociologically, politically, psychologically, spiritually, it was never enough for him [James Baldwin] to categorize himself as one thing or the other: not just black, not just sexual, not just American, nor even just as a world-class literary artist. He embraced the whole of life the way the sun's gravitational passion embraces everything from the smallest wandering comet to the largest looming planet. He both confronted and cultivated creative vision with a drive, passion, and brilliance that few have matched, and simply being able to watch his genius sparkle from one sentence to the next could generate both awe and revelation.
(UCI, The Quotable James Baldwin)

When we come to the literary art of Jean Toomer, we meet a poet similar to Langston Hughes in his love for the flowing rhythms of the blues and black folks' gospel, but quite different in his thematic approaches. Jean Toomer is a rarity among the black poets of his era because his poetic vision was not so much racial, political, or even social as it was

mystical and cosmic in scope. His sense of African-American destiny was linked as much to an awareness of universal forces as it was to an awareness of historical change.
(UCI, Traditions of Afrocentric Poetry for Georgia Poetry Society)

Because *Invisible Man* is a celebrated novel that has sold untold millions of copies in different languages around the world for more than half a century, the stories of cultural politics and extramarital dalliances surrounding its celebrity author may not stun readers too much. What might, though, while reading along, is the realization of just how much cultural and political influence Ellison came to wield based on the strength of that one mighty novel and a couple of volumes of essays.
(IC, The Enigmatic Genius of Ralph Ellison)

That tennis great Arthur Ashe died a victim of AIDS on February 6, 1993, is an undeniable tragedy. The fact that while he lived, he did so with consummate integrity, intelligence, and grace, remains his enduring legacy.
(UCI, The Amazing Grace of Arthur Ashe)

The best artists, like Langston Hughes himself, confront and battle with the worst realities until they are able to wrestle

from them meanings that add to the beauty of life instead of
enabling them to magnify the agonies of life.
(IC, Text and Meaning in Langston Hughes' The Negro
Artist and the Racial Mountain)

Woody Allen is a film master of complex character studies
and social entanglements that lend themselves to
philosophically absurd interpretations.
(UCI, Three Reasons to Celebrate Woody Allen: Vicky
Cristina Barcelona)

A major component of the Maxwell's success from the
beginning has been a spiritual quality within his music that
enhanced its appeal to no small degree.
(IC, The Nujazz New Millennium Soul of Maxwell's
BLACKsummers'night)

The Consecrated Soul of Whitney Houston
(August 9, 1963 – February 11, 2012)
(*complete poem*)

Your greatest hit is your consecrated soul,
notes dipped in gold by the one who made you.

Your style could burn valentine-heart red,
or smolder soulfully brilliant, ingeniously blue.

Sometimes on wings of diamond soprano,
or then again on comets of billion-dollar contralto...
you flew heights profoundly sacred—
one moment adored, the next embattled.

With blood flowing from gospel's rock of ages,
you sang the world's fury into rose-scented grace.
Time dressed you in gowns of astonished majesty;
starlight blessed you with an angel's glittering face.

Who among humans are equipped to judge you?
Many still squint trying to glimpse your light.
Beauty from another world gave birth to your voice—
sent to rescue scorned hearts from traumatized nights.

Your greatest hit is your consecrated soul,
notes dipped in gold by the one who made you.
Gently now, eternity engraves your name with hymns,
weeping ballads of love—and psalms of gratitude.
(AAC, Notebook on Black History Month 2012 (part 6): The
Consecrated Soul of Whitney Houston)

12. History Then and Now

Ancestral memory can be a strange thing that at times feels
more like ancestral empathy.
(GFO, Greeting Flannery O'Connor at the Back Door of My
Mind)

At one end of the continuum known as history are first-time
events that have generated notable measures of public
recognition due to either a positive or negative impact. At
the other end of the spectrum are individuals, organizations,
and occurrences which have earned acknowledgment due to
their enduring longevity and lasting influence upon humanity.
(AAC, Countdown 10 Amazing Moments in the Year
2011launches this week)

Nation-building is never a "done deal" confined to history already established. It is a perpetual one that requires the safeguarding and empowerment of citizens—all of them—in exchange for the loyalty, cooperation, and contributions that ensure a country's ongoing growth and cohesion.
(IC, Trayvon Martin, Robert Lee, and millions of tears fallen)

The single almost universally recognized event that set the tone and theme for the first decade of American history in the 21st century was the bombing of the World Trade Center in New York City on September 11, 2001.
(IC, Countdown of 10 Amazing Moments from the Year 2011: No. 2 President Barack Obama)

Courage can make human beings astonishingly beautiful and one can see such beauty in news films of freedom marchers, black and white, from the 1960s.
(IC, Why I Cried When Barack Obama Received the Democratic Nomination for President of the United States)

In a Global Village where connectivity via social networks has all but erased geographical boundaries, they reject the idea that they must live in perpetual poverty and cultural isolation in order to remain true to their faith.
(UCI, As Egypt Howls and History Tweets)

In many ways Hip-hop is the Harlem Renaissance of the
twenty-first century.
(IC, The Harlem Renaissance Hip-hop Connection)

Ours is an age in which entire biographies are frequently
reduced to thumb-sized apps or 140-character Twitter tweets.
The good news about this 21st century development is that it
has fostered communication and a sense of human
interconnectedness on unprecedented personal, community,
national, and international levels. The not-so-good downside
is that it trains our attention spans to shrink to ridiculous
capacities.
(IC, Barack Obama and the message beyond the photograph)

Wind of April 15, 2007, screeching like knives on fire.
Wind of April 16, 2007, in Virginia 33 counted dead.
(RWD, All Night in Savannah The Wind Wrote Poetry)

The end of legalized slavery did more than provide liberation
for the bodies of some four million slaves by the time the
Civil War ended. It also provided a kind of freedom for the
minds and souls of those Whites who for whatever reason
had believed that slavery was a sustainable institution in a
society founded precisely to restrict limitations imposed upon
individual human liberty.
(IC, Notes on the 150th Anniversary of the Emancipation
Proclamation)

The concept of freedom has to be one of the most finely-crafted double-edged swords humankind has ever created. On the one hand, it gleams with the jewel studs of what many like to consider are humanity's most noble qualities—individuality, courage, creativity, and integrity. On the other, it dims the light of any hope for sustained joy in the world when taken to extremes that impinge not only upon the "rights" of others but that destroy their actual lives and any sense of freedom embodied by those lives.
(UCI, On Freedom)

September 11, 2001: Citizens of the U.S., besieged by terror's sting,
rose up, weeping glory, as if on eagles' wings.
(RWD, Angel of Remembrance: Candles for September 11, 2001)

The memory and impact of 9/11
is something living generations
will take with them to their graves,
so it's right and natural that we should always honor those
murdered on that day
and continue to combat both terrorism
and its causes until humanity
no longer feels the need to resort
to violence to resolve its differences.
(UCI, MySpace Artists Interview with Nhojj)

Certainly with the enslavement of their parents and
grandparents less than seventy years behind them, the odds
of successfully utilizing black culture to better refine the
application of democracy in America was against them. Yet
the planners and participants in this would-be renaissance
moved forward with all the faith and visionary certainty of
Betsy Ross stitching the American flag or General William T.
Sherman blazing a trail of victory through the Civil War
South.
(AP, Encyclopedia of the Harlem Renaissance Author's note)

Politicians and activists during the 1960s made this important
observation: the U.S. Congress can legislate on the propriety
or impropriety of public conduct but it cannot legislate or
command the qualities of an individual's heart, mind, or soul.
That is a job which only the individual can do.
(IC, Obama, the Tea Party, and the Art of Political
Persuasions)

With Kennedy's assassination, Americans witnessed how
human beings sometimes force upon history reference points
defined by horror.
(IC, Text and Meaning in Robert Frost's "Dedication: For
John F. Kennedy)

American women, like so many others around the world,
were trained largely to live as second-class citizens, and living
as a second-class citizen meant living as a victim. It was only

by empowering them with full social and economic equality
that average mothers, wives, and daughters of the world
stood a chance of providing for themselves and the offspring
they bore.
(WD, Women)

When reading about what may be described as the lesser
celebrated heroic figures of the Harlem Renaissance, we
rarely get a definitive look at just how complicated and
sometimes dangerous their everyday lives were. In fact, until
the past ten years, many defined the period primarily by its
well-known literary, musical, and artistic elements while
overlooking the fact there was any political component to it
at all.
(UCI, A Forgotten Poet Gets His Due Review of The Great
Debaters)

Think of African Americans leaving slavery behind to be
counted among their country's most esteemed war veterans,
inventors, business people, educators, creative artists, and
leaders. Think of women stepping beyond the kitchen and
bedroom to increase the strength of their homeland on
battlefields and in corporations and government with their
individual and collective courage and genius. (RR, Between
the Waning Moons of 2008 and the Rising Suns of 2009)

While the enslavement of African Americans was an
unavoidable historical fact, so was the historical record of

their courage in the face of mortal danger, their strength
before seemingly insurmountable odds, their faith when
confronted with conditions that had driven others to faithless
despair, and their evocation of beauty and genius under
oppressive circumstances that did not encourage either.
(WD, African Americans)

The story of the American Civil War is essentially one of
human beings—Northerners, Southerners, Blacks, Whites,
men, women— holding themselves accountable for the
future of a nation. Some did so with informed ideas about
what their individual choices could or would mean; others did
so with little awareness, or at least little regard for the larger
moral, economic, or political implications.
(GFO, Dreams of the Immortal City)

The job facing American voters… in the days and years to
come, is to determine which hearts, minds, and souls
command those qualities best suited to unify a country rather
than further divide it, to heal the wounds of a nation as
opposed to aggravate its injuries, and to secure for the next
generation a legacy of choices based on informed awareness
rather than one of reactions based on unknowing fear.
(IC, Obama, the Tea Party, and the Art of Political
Persuasions)

Struggle against seemingly insurmountable odds has been a hallmark of African-American existence since the days of slavery. Despite these odds and ongoing adverse conditions, African Americans have continued to contribute substantially to the culture, strength, and preservation of the United States as a whole.
(AAC, Countdown of 10 Great Moments in African-American History 2010 Part 1)

History sometimes leaves humanity no choice except to respect the nature of that reality known as change.
(IC, Text and Meaning in Robert Frost's "Dedication: For John F. Kennedy)

13. Time and Change

Life decrees its own logic and is generally unmindful of what individual human beings do or do not make of it in regard to its eternal progressions.
(AP, With Love: A Letter from Yesterday to the Present and the Future)

With or without a political mandate to add to their impact, changes big and small are ongoing features of what we call our human condition.
(RR, Between the Waning Moons of 2008 and the Rising Suns of 2009)

The Internet, as valiantly represented in the media by Twitter, Facebook, and other social networks did not create the new century but has played a major role in the evolved vision of possibilities for this century.
(AAC, As Egypt Howls and History Tweets)

Time (again, Time) like the soul, wears many faces, many bodies and climates and attitudes. The past is one face, the present a second and the future yet another.
(IMBP, Past Present and Future Are One)

Whether we consider Hip-hop as an evolved manifestation of the Harlem Renaissance or something completely new under the sun, it clearly has moved beyond the stage of just entertaining lives to that of informing and empowering lives.
(IC, The Harlem Renaissance Hip-hop Connection)

As humanity's urgencies and priorities continue to change, I note the lesson of the dinosaurs.
(IC, Introduction)

Historians the world over will take a new inventory of the centuries behind us and futurists will contemplate the landscapes of those in front us.
(RR, Between the Waning Moons of 2008 and the Rising Suns of 2009)

A bridge of silver wings stretches from the dead ashes of an
unforgiving nightmare
to the jeweled vision of a life started anew.
(RWD, The River of Winged Dreams)

The fierce urgency of this moment is as much about
Humanity's need to transform ideas regarding love and
compassion into acts of love and compassion as it is about
demonstrating the ability to overcome cultural and racial
differences for the sake of unify in times of crisis.
(IC, The Fierce Urgency of This Moment)

Change is one of the scariest things in the world and yet it is
also one of those variables of human existence that no one
can avoid.
(GD, Dancing to the Paradigm Rhythms of Change in
Action)

It's not the physical distance from one town to another town,
or even from one country to another country that makes the
journey home so difficult. It is struggling to traverse that
emotional distance between the individuals we once were,
and those individuals we have somehow become.
(UCI, Joyous Day: Authenticity or Appropriation

I once watched Time grow fat
then explode in my face
as if too much pain
or too much love had gathered too fast
into a single small space.
(EPL, Washington Park #162)

A big part of the fun of entering a New Year is making a list
of noble resolutions, some of which we work hard to keep
and some of which become lost causes shortly after midnight
on New Year's Eve.
(UCI, Tagging Books and Authors to Watch in 2008)

Consider the labors of those extraordinary founding fathers
and mothers who foresaw the need for a constitution capable
of absorbing, accommodating, and even fostering all manner
of one thing: change.
(RR, Between the Waning Moons of 2008 and the Rising
Suns of 2009)

As history has demonstrated many times over, change may
arrive slowly or quickly but it is the one constant, in one form
or another, on which we can all count.
(GD, Dancing to the Paradigm Rhythms of Change in
Action)

Shaping and packaging and then re-shaping and re-packaging
how we relate to one another have turned social networkers
into millionaires and billionaires.
(IC, Poetics of Paradigm Dancing in the 2012 Presidential
Election Campaign)

> Time to be the sun
> and send forth flesh
> to heal the bones of time.
> (IMBP, Time to be the Sun)

This rose of pearl-coated infinity transforms
the diseased slums of a broken heart
into a palace made of psalms and gold.
(VS, Gratitudes of a Dozen Roses)

Somewhere inside my emptiness time is just beginning.
And somewhere inside my nowhere time has already ended.
(VS, The Drawing of the Two Dervishes)

The nature of modern technology, however, is that nothing
stays exactly the same for very long. Therefore…adapt, apply,
and move forward.
(UCI, from Catching up With Kindle and Company)

Time is a wizard that can pull either agony or ecstasy out of its magical hat, depending solely on the hand behind the heart within the eyes that gleam. Then fade.
(EPL, Past Present and Future are One)

14. Humanity and Hope

Hearts rebuilt from hope resurrect dreams killed by hate.
(RWD, Angel of Healing)

Freedom as one component of a given society does not guarantee joy, success, or peace of mind. What it offers is opportunity to identify and achieve such goals.
(IC, Notes on the 150th Anniversary of the Emancipation Proclamation)

Even greater than the ability to inspire others with hope is the power to motivate them to give as much to the lives of others as they would give to their own; and to empower them to confront the worst in themselves in order to discover and claim the best in themselves.
(UCI: In Honor of Oprah Winfrey)

History dressed up in the glow of love's kiss turned grief into beauty.
(RWD, Angel of Remembrance)

Light of angelic eyes shine faith, speak compassion, bring love.
(VS, Angel for New Orleans)

Between the hopelessness of despair capable of destroying a life, and the strength that comes with self-assurance capable of empowering a life, there sits a great chasm with which many people struggle when attempting to cross from one side to the other. (RWD, Deliverance in Action)

Big problems call for big solutions that often require serious work and commitment but which are not impossible to accomplish.
(IC, Notes on the 150th Anniversary of the Emancipation Proclamation)

Souls reconstructed with faith transform agony into peace.
(RWD, Angel of Healing)

And now we step to the rhythm of miracles.
(IMBP, The Light, That Never Dies)

I would say that Love is the only hope the world has of
overcoming its predilection for mass suicide, but that would
not be true. Almost all of our religions, many of our forms
of government, philosophies, science, art, and social
organizations could save the human race if all of mankind
were to give its heart to that single goal.
(AP, With Love a Letter from Yesterday to the Present and
the Future)

In the days when hyenas of hate suckle the babes of men, and
jackals of hypocrisy pimp their mothers' broken hearts, may
children not look to demons of ignorance for hope.
(RWD, A Coat and Shoes for Halloween)

This crying for the world can wear your ass out… We can cry
for years but sometimes gotta smile too.
(VS, Louie the Madman Cries for the World)

Cradled in scorched arms,
a soldier's moon keeps its vows—
shines persistent hope.
(RWD, Angel of Hope's Persistent Flight)

The best of humanity's recorded history is a creative balance between horrors endured and victories achieved, and so it was during the Harlem Renaissance. (RR)

In an age when nations and individuals routinely exchange murder for murder, when the healing grace of authentic spirituality is usurped by the divisive politics of religious organizations, and when broken hearts bleed pain in darkness without the relief of compassion, the voice of an exceptional poet producing exceptional work is not something the world can afford to dismiss.
(AP, Visions of the Poets: Andre Emmanuel Bendavi ben-YEHU)

As life in general constituted much pain in the form of struggles against poverty, disease, ignorance, and emotional anguish, what more civilized way for people to alleviate the same than by giving themselves to one another as brothers and sisters in deed as well as in word? A society of people hoping to become politically superior needed first to become spiritually valid.
(WD, Civilization and Human Nature)

Holy jazzmen of small mystic hours
blow ye furious the rainbow of hope.
(RWD, An Angel for New Orleans)

Between death and hell a bridge shining silver wings offers
his soul hope.
(RWD, Angel of Better Days to Come)

Without access to the varied forms of education suitable for
every individual temperament and every class of worker, the
potential for continued growth and securing an authentically
functional democracy in the United States decreased
considerably. More than a means to a substantial paycheck,
both education and satisfying work were the means to a
substantial character.
(WD, Work and Education)

Death wins nothing here,
gnawing wings that amputate—
then spread, lift up, fly.
(RWD, Angel of Hope's Persistent Flight)

Source and Subject Index

Index entries indicating the titles of books, poems, articles, or other works in which a quote first appeared are followed by an abbreviation of the title of the original source in parentheses. The source key is in the front section of the book just before the introduction.

0

2012

A

Ralph Ellison
Hill Harper
Langston Hughes
Zora Neale Hurston
Juan Ramon Jimenez, vi
Franz Kafka, 78
Jack Kerouac
Gary Loper
Dambudzo Marechera
Toni Morrison
Flannery O'Connor
Ben Okri
Rainer Maria Rilke
Jalal al-Din Rumi
William Shakespeare
Jean Toomer
Boris Vian

B

D

I

J

K

L

N

O

V

W

Author-Poet Aberjhani (photo © by John Zeuli)

About the Author

A native of Savannah, Georgia (U.S.A.), Aberjhani has been an internationally-known author since 1997 when his writings first began to appear in *ESSENCE Magazine*. Some 15 years and almost as many books later—as an author, poet, editor, historian, and journalist—Google search engines began to place him among those "Authors frequently mentioned on the web."

Readers around the world have come to recognize him as a multi-talented writer of creative nonfiction, ground-breaking history, luminously-charged poetry, speculative fiction, and a singular brand of interpretive journalism. They also know him as an advocate, for both the cultural arts and human rights, who founded the popular *Creative Thinkers International* social network in 2007 and the *100th Anniversary of the Harlem Renaissance Initiative* in 2013.

As an online columnist, he has provided opinion-shaping commentaries on some of the most crucial issues of modern times, from Arab Spring and the life and death of Michael Jackson to the 2012 U.S. presidential election campaign and the struggle for human rights throughout the Global Village. Commentators have described him as "a poet of conscience and a critic of injustice in contemporary society."

He can be counted among a handful of authors whose work has garnered awards in several major categories. They include: The Choice Academic Title Award, the Thomas Jefferson

Journalism Award, the Michael Jackson Tribute Portrait VIP
Dot Award, Best History Book Award, Best Poet and Spoken
Word Artist Award, and Notable New Jersey Book of the
Year Award. He is well-known for his fellowship with various
cultural workers/creative artists and has been a consistent
supporter of the principles and ideals championed by
International PEN and the Academy of American Poets.